Personal Finance

Fortress

Getting A Clear Picture Of How To Set Up Budgeting Exercises

Terms and Conditions

Table Of Contents

Foreword

Budgeting may not necessarily be all about curbing all spending powers. It is only a suggested method of spending, that is both wise and that will keep the individual from falling into an all consuming debt ridden situation. Get all the info you need here.

Personal Finance Fortress
Getting A Clear Picture Of How To Set Up Budgeting Exercises

Chapter 1:

Personal Budgeting Basics

Synopsis

The following are some tips on how to successfully maintain a personal budgeting outline:

The Basics

Perhaps the first and most important act to commit to is the detailed tracking exercise of the expenses for the individual monthly commitments.

Creating a tracking system from the close scrutiny of bills collected over a three month period will help give the individual an idea of the general commitments to date.

By having this clearly listed and detailed the individual will be able to design a suitable budget that can be easily followed without the need to be too constrictive.

This budgeting exercise can take into account all expenses such as fixed commitments, periodic commitments, occasional treats and any other types of usual expenses calculated on a monthly basis.

Settings goals is also another type of personal budgeting element that should be included as a form of incentive to the individual. It is also a way to create discipline that will help the individual prepare for bigger commitments in the future. Setting goals will also help the individual have a better perspective on the future possibilities of investment opportunities.

The act to creating and adhering to a personal budget plan can also help the individual be disciplined in other fields too. This may contribute positively in other areas, such as job commitments, family commitments, retirement plans, investments and any other area that may require the same discipline that produces successful results always.

It will also help the individual to make wiser judgment calls, thus ensuring the possibility of getting in debts be kept at a minimum or even eliminated altogether.

Chapter 2:

Finance Plans That Allocates For Future Personal Income

Synopsis

Planning for the future, entails being knowledgeable in financial areas, which can create security and profits for future enjoyment. This will enable the individual to enjoy some level of comfort in the future without having to pursue additional income earning avenues.

The Future

The following are some steps that can be considered in pursuit of time goal:

Educating one's self on the various different personal investment schemes would be one way of going about securing the future of an individual's personal income.

There are many types of investments that can earn the individual a comfortable amount of profits that can be used as a source of income in the future.

Personal savings plans can also contribute to future income possibilities. However if this plan is not enforced in a committed fashion where access to the funds put away are either limited or nonexistent, then this style of savings will not benefit or be suitable as a future income source.

This is due to the fact that the accessibility will encourage the individual to make withdrawals frequently based on excuse possible.

Having a diversified portfolio of financial investments will also ensure the risk levels are kept to a minimum and that future income projected can be enjoyed.

Choosing long term investment tools are better, as they popularly provide better earning possibilities as compared to short term investment. These may include government bonds, insurance policies, bonds from reputable agencies and establishments.

Being able to accurately access financial investments against the primary risk tolerance of an individual is also something that should be given due consideration.

There is little point in starting an investment portfolio if the ability of service such investments are either nonexistent or unreliable.

All the above suggestions should also be calculated with the relevant tax incurring ratios that should ideally still make the investment worth venturing into.

Chapter 3:

How To Follow A Budget Plan

Synopsis

Following a budget plan is not impossible to do if the right tools and mindset is in place. There are a few true and tried methods that can help an individual design and successfully stick to the budget plan.

Following

The following are some recommendations as to how this can be achieved:

The first and most important act to exercise is the recording of all income and expense for the month. This should be diligently done over a period of at least three months consecutively.

Once these detailed itemized incoming and outgoing points are clearly recorded, then follow up measures can be incorporated into the budget plan to start the process that ensures the individual is well equipped to handle and stick to the plan drawn up.

There are several tools available that can help the individual in this style of tracking.

The next step would be to record only the income and very necessary expenses such as commitments towards loans, insurances, education payments and any others.

Ideally these should be calculated as a yearly expense and then divided to fit into the monthly expenditure plan. This will help the individual have a complete overview of his or her yearly commitments thus providing the means to make such payment in a more disciplined and affordable way.

At the end of the above exercises, it is hoped that the income is greater than the committed expenses. If this is found to be so, then the individual can enjoy the leeway of adding on other expenses that are not deemed necessary or vital to the healthy existence of the individual financial position.

These may include little indulgences such as an occasional expensive meal or personal treat. This will encourage the individual to stick to the budget planned as the possibility of ever being in debt is kept at bay.

Chapter 4:

Spreadsheet Budgeting With Date Shifting

Synopsis

Any budget is only as effective as the real time notations that are updated periodically. Having the correct assisting tools will help to make the process of spreadsheet budgeting and date shifting effective.

Spreadsheet

All spending both immediate and future is usually noted on the spreadsheet but this is not always fixed as adjustments are made accordingly as they unfold. The following are some of the tools and methods used to keep the spreadsheet updated:

Perhaps the most basic tools are the simple jotting down of information on paper to be entered into the spreadsheet when the periodic updating exercise is done.

There are also a lot of money management websites that can help to specifically assist in the money management program. These programs keep track of the all the accounts information which may include saving and other money generating accounts, and then make the necessary adjustments to display useful information for future budgeting.

With the help of the spreadsheet budgeting style, the individual is able to clearly note all payments and commitments at a glance. This is very helpful when trying to decide on the importance tagged to the payments.

If there are credit cards outstanding amounts the spreadsheet will help to highlight the cards that most need attention and if funds permit more money can be focused on paying the debts that have the highest interest rates.

The date shifting done on the information furnished by the spreadsheet will help create a better avenue of clearing the commitments that are either prioritized or cost more in terms of interest accrued. In some way the clarity of the figures shown in this way will create the urgency for the individual to focus on making the relevant payments in its priority form.

It will also give the individual a clear overview of his or her financial status both in the present and in the future if the necessary information is well documented and allocated.

Chapter 5:

Enjoying Life Without Busting The Bank

Synopsis

With careful planning and an income that does not fluctuate too much it is possible to be able to enjoy life in the present without having to chalk up a lot of debts. All it really takes is a little planning and discipline.

Enjoy

The following are some recommendation on how to go about this exercise:

Going on a vacation does not necessarily have to be done in opulent style. Look for alternatives that are similar and equally exciting that will fit into a budget that is available is a better way to plan and enjoy while all the time being firm about keeping within the budget.

The ability to plan within the budget will ensure no unnecessary debts are accumulated thus possibly creating the space to future better holidays, since the current one did not end up burdening the individual with debts that would have to be serviced along after the holiday is over.

Indulging periodically is also advised provided the exercise does not cost as exorbitant amount that will keep the individual in debt long after the enjoyment passes. However total abstinence can also negatively affect the individual as it may cause sudden over indulgence.

Looking for the best deals can not only be fun but also constitute to huge savings possibilities.

Learning to source for items in less convention ways such as garage sales and closing down sales will allow the individual to find items that are not overly prices and yet suited to the current needs. The latest platform that is fast gaining popularity is the online trading style where items are often bought for very low prices indeed.

Focusing on working on side incomes to help pay for indulgences is also another way to enjoy without incurring unnecessary debts. Taking on odd jobs and small project with the intention of using the money for a little pleasure is quite an encouraging tool to go by.

Chapter 6:

Tips On Putting Together A Complete Household Budget

Synopsis

Most people assume household budgets only consist of immediate expenses incurred within a month that are household expense related. However a complete household budget realistically takes into account all incoming and outgoing funds within the said household on an ideally yearly basis.

Tips

The following are some of the areas that are not conventionally addressed but should be done in the quest to have a complete household budget:

There should be a clear and accurate spreadsheet done on the house hold income. This is necessary when there are multiple sources of income, thus creating the need to have such details noted clearly.

There would also be a need to list the mandatory payments that are done within the monthly commitments. If there are any payments that are made in a fashion other than the usual monthly commitments, these payments have to be averaged out and included in the monthly commitment household budget.

Allotments should also be made for discretionary spending which usually covers any and all categories. The allotment should be of a comfortable amount without being over indulgent. This is to ensure there is still some level of discipline and control encompassing the household budget.

Savings are also to be included especially if they are in the context of being part of a commitment towards some sort of plan.

These may include savings for retirement, savings for emergency funds, savings for educational funds and any other long term style commitments that can fluctuate in its committed amounts for payment.

If there are any debts to be cleared, then the payments towards these should also be part of the household budget records. The payments for such existing debts will only be added on for the duration it takes to pay off such platforms.

Chapter 7:

Simple Tricks And Tips For Sticking To A Budget

Synopsis

For some people planning a budget is a fairly easy task to carry out, the ability to stick to the planned budget outlined is where the challenge starts. This challenge has often caused many individual to fail or falter in some way.

Easy Ways

The following are some tips to help keep this negative possibility from happening:

Drawing up a budget that is both realistic and clear is a good start to make. With this budget the individual is able to have something tangible to focus on and actually be aware of where the incoming and outgoing funds are heading.

Tracking the spending style will give the individual a better overview of how and where the money is being spent. For most this may be a surprisingly eye opening experience as most people don't keep track of the details of their spending habit and are therefore not really aware of just how frivolous some of the purchases made are.

Thus this tracking will help bring some semblance of sanity back into the spending style of the individual and hopefully curb further unnecessary indulgences.

Making it a habit to only use cash for any purchases whether small or large is something that should be adopted immediately. When there is an actual exchange of cash the transaction makes a bigger impact on the individual mindset.

Wrapping Up

One of the most effective methods to ensure a budget is consistently adhered to is to avoid putting one's self in a situation where the temptation to spend is hard to control. This would mean cutting down on window shopping sprees and other frivolous indulgences, until the individual is strong enough to do so without actually having to spend on anything. In some more drastic cases the individual may even have to resort to changing the circle of friends he or she hangs out with, if the said group prioritizes activities like shopping and other equally costly indulgences.

www.ingramcontent.com/pod-product-compliance
Lightning Source LLC
Chambersburg PA
CBHW041622180526
45159CB00002BC/970